CRAFTS
OF THE ANCIENT WORLD

THE CRAFTS AND CULTURE OF
THE ROMANS

Joann Jovinelly and Jason Netelkos

the rosen publishing group's
rosen
central

To Jenell, may you know the beauty of your ancient ancestry

2/03

Published in 2002 by The Rosen Publishing Group, Inc.
29 East 21st Street, New York, NY 10010

Library of Congress Cataloging-in-Publication Data

Jovinelly, Joann.
The crafts and culture of the Romans / Joann Jovinelly and Jason Netelkos.
p. cm. — (Crafts of the ancient world)
Includes bibliographical references and index.
Summary: Information about life in ancient Rome accompanies a variety of related craft projects. Also includes a timeline, a glossary, and other resources.
ISBN 0-8239-3513-2
1. Handicraft—Rome—Juvenile literature. 2. Rome—Social life and customs—Juvenile literature. [1. Rome—Social life and customs. 2. Handicraft.]
I. Title. II. Series.
TT16 .J68 2002
937—dc21

2001004719

Manufactured in the United States of America

Note to Parents
Some of these projects require tools or materials that can be dangerous if used improperly. Adult supervision will be necessary when projects require the use of a craft knife, an oven, a stovetop, plaster of paris, or pins and needles. Before starting any of the projects in this book, you may want to cover your work area with newspaper or plastic. In addition, we recommend using a piece of thick cardboard to protect surfaces while cutting with craft or mat knives. Parents, we encourage you to discuss safety with your children and note in advance which projects may require your supervision.

CONTENTS

The story of the birth and development of the ancient civilization of Rome is filled with tales of war, betrayal, conquest, triumph, and artistic achievement. At the height of their power, the Romans occupied a vast territory that extended from Britain to Arabia, stretching from the waters of the Atlantic Ocean to those of the Black Sea. Rome was a city filled with beautiful architecture, well-engineered roads, and innovative sewage systems. They even had indoor plumbing.

Many Roman advances were built on the earlier technological achievements of the Greeks, who were known for their exquisite artistic ability. Though highly influenced by Greek culture, the Romans made many important contributions of their own, some of which are still in use today, such as the Roman calendar. The fall of the Roman Empire is an equally interesting story and is usually attributed to a variety of

The she-wolf Capitoline nurses her sons Romulus and Remus.

factors that had their source in changes in Rome's political, social, and economic systems.

Legend has it that Rome was founded in 753 BC by twin brothers named Romulus and Remus, sons of the war god Mars, on seven hills bordered by the Tiber River. Romulus and Remus decided to each rule a section of the new city they would build. When Romulus laid out the boundaries of his section, Remus discovered that his brother's territory was much larger than his own. They fought, and Romulus killed Remus. Romulus then went on to build the city that got its name, Rome, from him. Eventually, Romulus was considered to be not only a god's son, but a god himself. This myth was an effort to gain respect for Rome by linking its founding to the gods.

In actuality, the area known as Rome was settled by groups of farmers and shepherds around the same period as that described in the founding myth.

During the height of the Roman Empire, its lands extended from Britain to Arabia, from the Atlantic Ocean to the Black Sea, as shown in this map dating from 1595.

Some were nomadic, which meant that they traveled from place to place. The area known as Italy was populated by a variety of different people who spoke different languages and were distinguished by various skills and customs. At the same time, other surrounding lands in the Mediterranean, such as Greece and Spain, were composed of numerous independent city-states—self-governing areas comprising a large town and, in many cases, its adjacent villages.

Some of these farmers were Etruscan, settlers who had lived in Italy since around 1100 BC, more than a thousand years before the rise of the Roman Empire. They had large extended families, and became more powerful than their fellow settlers. They were considered the owners of the land they farmed and were known as Roman citizens, or patricians—a privileged class. At some point, these citizens came together to choose officials who would represent them and their interests. The elected officials eventually began to rule as kings, of which there were seven.

These seven kings governed early Roman society before the city-state became a republic governed by a group of nonroyal elected officials. The new Roman republican government included

5

two consuls, who organized military forces and helped to enforce decisions, and senators, elected officials who made decisions in the Senate, a law-making institution. These changes took place in 509 BC, setting the stage for the impressive growth that followed and allowed Rome to extend its reach far into Europe, Asia, the Middle East, and Africa.

Public officials often did a poor job of representing all the republic's people, since many Romans were poor and all of the government officials were patricians elected to office by other patricians. The vast group of plebians—the most common group of Roman citizens, which included the poor and middle class—were often not shown enough consideration by this ruling class. In times of trouble, such as during a war, the democratic process could be abandoned altogether. During a crisis, the Senate could elect a dictator who had absolute power over all of Rome and its citizens.

DAILY LIFE

Roman lifestyles were dictated almost entirely by the social class to which a person belonged. These classes included the rich and the poor, and citizens and noncitizens. The lowest possible class within Roman society was that of the slave. As the Roman Empire became larger and more powerful, the Senate placed increased demands upon its people, especially the poorer classes and the slaves. Sometimes these demands were in the form of tariffs, or taxes. Most people were common laborers; very few enjoyed the life of luxury usually associated with Rome's sophisticated and advanced culture.

The citizen class was divided into three categories: those who were senators, those who were descendants of the first Roman army officials (equestrians), and the rest of the free people. Roman citizens (originally only those people who were born in the city of Rome) had many privileges. Citizens could vote in elections, take a job within the government, and seek entertainment at the public games that took place at the Colosseum, Rome's huge public amphitheater. They were also entitled to an allowance of free grain that was made into bread and distributed as loaves. Finally, citizens, unlike slaves and other noncitizens, could join the Roman army. As the Roman Empire grew, people from outside the city of Rome (provincials) were finally considered citizens, too. This law included all of Italy by AD 212.

In contrast to the many rights provided to Rome's citizenry, slaves—both male and female—had no rights at all. Many worked for wealthy

This reconstruction of a Roman villa at Pompeii includes the main atrium and a number of small, private rooms, which can be seen on either side.

Roman families and lived in separate quarters. Most slaves were born into slavery as the children of other slaves, and many worked as musicians, artisans, and craftspeople. Occasionally a slave could buy his or her freedom. In other instances, slaves could win the right to be free by publicly fighting for it. These demonstrations of public fighting took place in the Colosseum with gladiators, specially trained fighters who often fought to the death using only swords and shields. A slave who fought successfully for his or her freedom in this way was known as a freedman or a freedwoman. Freedmen and freedwomen had fewer rights than citizens did but were allowed to own land and businesses. This group became the heart of Rome's middle-class society, and their children were considered full citizens. Overall, the work ethic in ancient Rome was a strong one, but most of its wealthy subjects took advantage of the poorer classes, which eventually contributed to the downfall of their civilization.

As in our own society, wealth played a large part in determining the quality of a Roman family's living quarters. Men and women married (though most marriages were arranged

These are the latrines of the Hadrianic baths in Libya. The Romans were the first people to build public toilets.

one mishap. The apartments themselves were confined quarters with windows facing streets that were often littered with garbage and other waste. They were noisy and had few of the conveniences that wealthy Romans enjoyed, such as indoor plumbing. By contrast, Rome's elite lived in much quieter, more beautiful surroundings. Wealthy families resided in villas (townhouses) that had many adornments, such as mosaic tiled floors, gardens, pools, and even, in some cases, a primitive form of centralized heating.

Regular Roman citizens ate a basic diet that included more grains than meat. They wore traditional togas (noncitizens could not wear togas and instead wore tunics—long shirts that were tied at the waist). They also enjoyed many forms of public entertainment, such as chariot racing, gladiator fighting, animal sacrificing, and athletics. It was common for all classes to mix at the *thermae* (public bathhouses) that were situated all over the empire. These buildings featured both hot and cold rooms, saunas, and pools, and often also included reading and exercise rooms and shops. Most Romans thought of the bathhouses as places of social activity.

for financial or political reasons rather than for love), had children, and lived within a tightly knit family unit. The father was considered the most powerful person in the Roman household and the literal owner of his family (and slaves if he had them). Most middle-class and poor families lived in *insula* (apartment buildings) that were situated over bustling shops. These buildings were often threatened by fire or collapse, and since they stood so closely together, a whole city block could be destroyed in

BELIEFS

The Romans were pagans who worshiped hundreds of gods and goddesses. People were expected to present offerings to them, sometimes in the form of animal or human sacrifices. There were gods who were considered helpful for healing the sick, offering protection from danger, or watching over the actions of children. The Romans often observed nature to interpret how the gods felt about their behavior. The eating habits of animals, the weather, or the way the sky and clouds appeared all seemed to indicate a certain attitude, mood, or message from the gods.

The most important and popular god in Rome was Jupiter, the god of the sky. The Romans often adopted gods from other cultures, too, such as the Egyptian goddess Isis, or the Greek goddess Athena. Gods were worshiped in large temples that were built throughout the empire. Inside each temple was a statue of the god to whom the temple was dedicated. Although there were Christians in Rome during the height of the empire, they were not allowed to practice their religion openly since Christianity was outlawed by the emperors. For the most part, Christianity was tolerated for centuries before Emperor Constantine converted to Christianity in AD 325 and established it as the state religion. The earlier emperors sometimes persecuted Christians, however, if they felt that their neglect of the pagan rites had offended the gods.

Roman emperors were often thought of as gods after their deaths, and sometimes temples were built to honor them. An altar just outside the entrance to the temple was where sacrifices were offered during worship services. In addition to animals, sacrifices could include pieces of precious jewelry, coins, food, and drink. Only priests could enter the inside of a temple, which was considered sacred. Romans also worshiped inside their homes. Every Roman household contained a shrine called a *lararium*.

The average life span of a person living in ancient Rome was short, probably only about thirty to fifty years, since many people fell victim to deadly diseases. Because of their beliefs that the gods could cause illness, disease, and other afflictions, many Romans sought miracle cures. Some traveled to distant spas hoping to find solutions to whatever diseases ailed them. Many placed small votive offerings upon the temple altars while praying to the gods for a cure.

Roman legionnaires load a catapult in this historical reenactment.

WARFARE

The Roman army was among the best in the entire ancient world. Its success stemmed from several key elements, including the ability to travel great distances. The army organized thousands of men into different units and invented advanced machinery, such as the ballista (catapult), which could launch stones as heavy as 220 pounds. In fact, it is widely accepted that the Roman Empire grew to cover such a large territory because of the organization and dedication of its army, then called the Roman Legionary.

Each section of the army, or legion, included about 5,000 foot soldiers called the infantry. These soldiers were highly disciplined and exceptionally well trained. During the height of Rome's power, these soldiers were treated very well and given large salaries. Eventually, after many generations of arming themselves with whatever they could afford, Roman soldiers began to receive equipment that was standardized.

The Roman army's first great success occurred around 260 BC when the empire, which contained all of present-day Italy, began a prolonged war (the Punic Wars, 264–146 BC) with Carthage, a North African state. Rome finally won the long campaign and gained its first overseas territory. Afterward, the army set its sights on other neighboring lands and the empire grew steadily. Under the leadership of Julius Caesar, the Roman Empire gained territories in North Africa and Gaul (a territory containing the present-day countries of France, Switzerland, Belgium, and parts of Germany). The murder of Julius Caesar—a powerful leader who declared himself Rome's dictator—in 44 BC signified the end of the Roman republic and the beginning of its downfall, which was slow but steady.

LANGUAGE

Throughout the entire history of the Roman Empire, the predominant language in use was Latin, although many people still preferred to speak and write in the Greek language, from which the Latin alphabet originated. The language of this period is usually described as "early Latin" (archaic Latin) and "classical" or "Golden Age" Latin.

The everyday speech of most Romans who spoke Latin differed from the Latin reserved for speeches, literature, proclamations, and official documents. This oral, more casual form of the language became the basis for other European languages, such as French and Italian, which are known as romance languages due to their Roman origins.

Most educated Romans learned Greek from an early age. Greek was commonly spoken throughout the empire and frequently appears in many Roman books and papyri. Other languages, such as Celtic, Punic, and Syriac, were also in use within the empire at the time.

ART

The ancient Greeks are celebrated for their artistic talent and innovation, whereas the ancient Romans are often thought of as skilled imitators. Greek culture inspired much of the art and architecture that was created by Roman artisans.

Public art was important to the Romans. Many examples may still be seen throughout Europe and in museum collections around the world, such as commissioned sculptures of deities (gods and goddesses), or famous, powerful, or wealthy citizens and emperors who were worshiped as gods. Perhaps the greatest Roman contributions to the world of art were its architectural and engineering innovations, such as the invention of the dome. The Romans were also the first civilization to build tall public buildings thanks to the introduction of concrete, which back then was a mixture of volcanic material and cement.

The Romans were also known for the finely designed interiors of their homes. Wealthy Romans often had villas that were decorated with mosaic tiled floors and walls, marble, inlaid woods (which were imported from other areas within the empire), and detailed frescoes (wall murals). Even Romans from the lower classes decorated their homes with frescoes, which are paintings applied directly to plaster walls.

Fashion

Fashion provided Roman society with one of its most enduring icons: the toga. It was worn consistently, with very little variation, throughout the period of the Roman Empire. Originally worn alone, the toga was later worn with an undergarment, the tunic—a long shirt, tied at the waist and worn mostly by slaves and the lower classes. Children wore tunics at all times and usually kept a *bulla*—a rounded charm, about the size of a seashell—around their necks. It was thought to provide both girls and boys with divine protection.

The white toga was the most common attire, but other colored togas were worn at special times, such as during a funeral when it was customary to don a black garment. The toga was very heavy and it required constant cleaning. Sometimes, chalk would be rubbed in its folds in order to make it appear whiter in color. Roman senators wore white togas that were bordered with purple trim, which

This is a statue of Augustus, the first emperor of Rome.

was either narrow or wide depending upon their position in government. Togas were made of either wool or linen and were fastened with a brooch called a fibula, a sort of safety pin usually made from a precious metal, such as gold.

Women wore togas just as men did. However, married women wore a long, ankle-length tunic called a *stola*, with a shawl called a *palla* draped over the toga. Both men and woman commonly wore sandals made of leather. In colder climates, pants would occasionally be worn, too, but this was not a common fashion style.

Besides the long, draping toga, women adorned their bodies with beautiful gold jewelry—earrings, necklaces, and rings that looked very much like today's jewelry does. They also dabbed a spice called saffron on the lids of their eyes and powdered their faces white, as pale-colored skin was much more fashionable than more tanned skin tones. Hair was pulled up and away from the face, sometimes in tiny braids, and sometimes fastened with a fabric headband.

Men's hair fashions changed throughout the years, too, but most men shaved their beards and cut their hair in short styles. Laurel leaves were worn on the head solely by emperors, and then only rarely, in order to signal to the Roman people that they had won a military battle or an equivalent achievement. The laurel wreath was symbolic of success and power and was not misused or worn frequently.

This bust of a woman dates from the Flavian dynasty (AD 69–96). Her braided and fastened hair was typical of Roman hairstyles for women.

In this portrait, Julius Caesar wears a laurel crown and brooch.

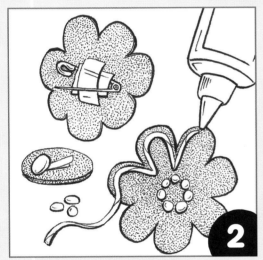

Toga, Brooch, and Laurel Crown

There is an old saying, "When in Rome, do as the Romans do." Recreate your own Roman wardrobe in a few easy steps.

YOU WILL NEED
- Cardboard
- Scissors
- Large safety pins
- Masking tape
- White glue
- String
- Paper fasteners
- Beads (optional)
- Gold craft paint
- Paint brush
- Pencil or pen
- Flat, white bedsheet
- Long string or rope (to wear as a belt)
- Pipe cleaners
- Paper
- Green paint or markers

Step 1
To make your brooch, draw a flower, slightly larger than your safety pin, on a small piece of cardboard. Cut out the design with your scissors. Roll the tips of the petals around a pencil so they curl up.

Step 2
Glue a safety pin to the back of the flower with white glue. Tape it in place until it is dry. Decorate the flower with glued pieces of string and paper fasteners. After they dry, paint the brooch gold.

Step 3
To make your toga, use a flat bedsheet of any size. A white sheet looks best, but any color sheet will do. Drape and gather the sheet from its midpoint over one shoulder and allow it to fall in folds down your back and across your chest. Pin it in place on your opposite shoulder. Tie a rope around your waist as a belt. Many Romans wore tunics under their togas, but a long white T-shirt will do, as well as white pants and simple sandals if you have them.

Step 4
To make the laurel crown, join and twist together the ends of two pipe cleaners. Form the pipe cleaners into a circular shape and fasten the other two ends.

Step 5

Fold a piece of paper in half. Cut out leaf shapes with thick stems along the fold. Make enough paper leaves to completely go around your pipe cleaner band. Color the leaves in various shades of green.

Step 6

Attach the leaves to the band with a small dab of white glue between the stems. Fold the first leaf under the wire band and glue it in place. Fold the second leaf over the wire and glue. Continue to add leaves, some pointing out from the band, and some inward in an alternating pattern. This will create a realistic layered effect. Adjust the leaves after they have dried until you are happy with their arrangement.

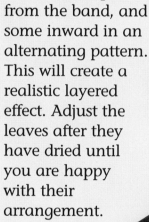

Romans at Home

Even wealthy Romans had very little furniture in their homes, but almost every room was decorated lavishly with art on its walls and floors. This art took the form of mosaic floor tiling and fresco wall painting. Wealthy Romans could also afford to import all sorts of expensive building materials which became a status symbol; often, the homes of government officials were finished in marble accents, detailed wooden moldings, and beautiful murals.

The constant demand for art of this sort helped to keep many Roman slaves busy from dawn until dusk creating mosaic pictures with small glass, stone, or clay tiles called tesserae, which were inserted into a wet mixture of plaster over concrete. The variously colored tiles were arranged together to create patterns or images.

This is a restoration of the interior of a Roman villa that once stood near Mount Vesuvius.

Mosaics served many purposes in ancient Rome. One home that remains standing in Pompeii, the ancient city that was destroyed by a volcanic eruption in AD 79, used a mosaic picture in its doorway to warn visitors about a fierce dog that awaited them upon entering. Its Latin inscription, *Cave Canem*, is a common phrase that we still use today: "Beware of dog!"

Nearly every Roman home was decorated using the ancient techniques of mosaic tiling, depicting everything from realistic scenes of everyday life, to fantastic images drawn from Roman and Greek mythology, to still-life arrangements of fruit and vegetables. Elaborate decorative displays became a person's testament to his or her financial or social status, announcing to all visitors the homeowner's standing in society. Mosaics began with the insertion of small pebbles into mud during the fifth century BC. Some of the best examples of this ancient artwork may be seen in the pavements of the city of Ostia in central Italy, near Rome, and in the figural compositions of Piazza Armerina in Sicily.

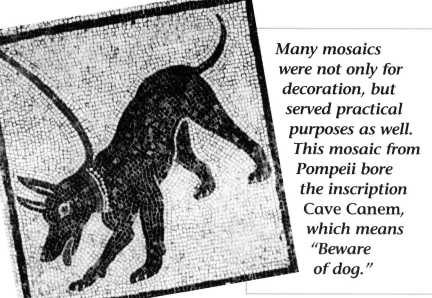

Many mosaics were not only for decoration, but served practical purposes as well. This mosaic from Pompeii bore the inscription Cave Canem, which means "Beware of dog."

This majestic mosaic floor is from Roman ruins in Morocco.

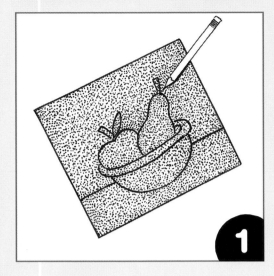

Mosaic Tile

Take some decorating tips from the Romans and design your very own mosaic tile.

YOU WILL NEED
- Pasta "beads"
- Craft paint
- Paintbrushes
- Pencil
- Cardboard
- White glue
- Paper towels
- Varnish

Step 1
Paint a piece of cardboard a dark shade, such as brown. When the paint dries, draw the picture you would like to mosaic with a pencil.

Step 2
Insert the end of a thin paintbrush through some of your pasta pieces. This will make them easier to paint. Paint the pieces in whatever colors you desire. Paint enough beads to fill in the entire surface of the cardboard.

Step 3
After all the paint on the beads dries completely, crack them by placing them on a hard, flat surface and pressing down on them with your thumb. After the beads break apart, the pieces will resemble the tiny mosaic tiles called tesserae.

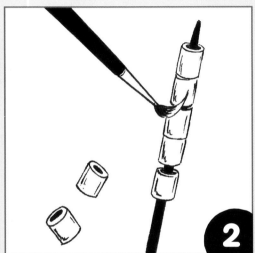

Step 4
Separately glue each tile to your cardboard with a small drop of white glue. Lightly press the tile onto the cardboard until it is firmly in place.

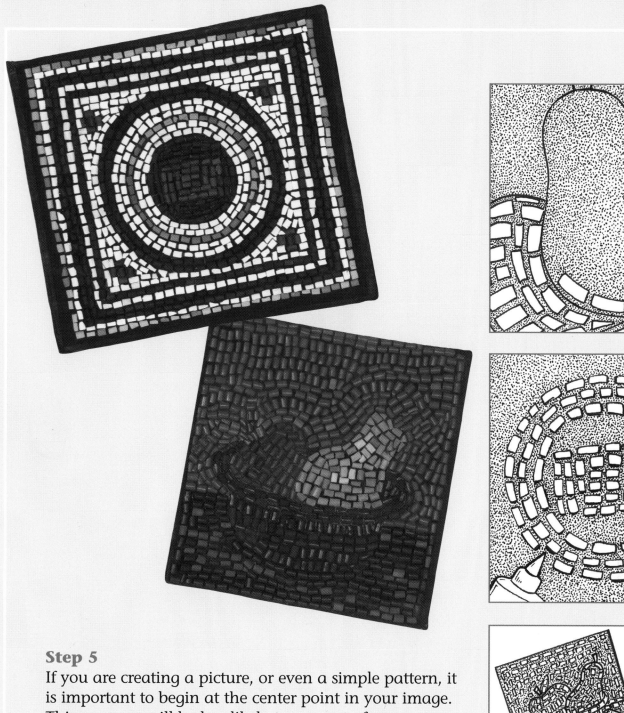

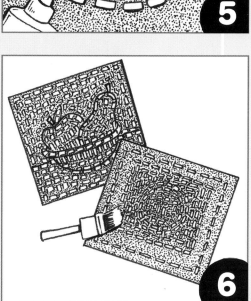

Step 5

If you are creating a picture, or even a simple pattern, it is important to begin at the center point in your image. This way you will be less likely to run out of space before the image is finished.

Step 6

After you have completed your picture, allow it to dry overnight. If you wish, you can add a coat of clear picture varnish (available at most hardware or craft stores) to make your mosaic appear shiny. If not, you could also use the remaining paint to touch up your tesserae.

Writing and Literature

In the early part of Rome's history, most children were educated at home by their fathers, who taught them basic reading, writing, and, in some cases, arithmetic. Toward the third century BC, however, the Romans began to institute systematic methods of teaching its citizens. Centered mainly on the study of Latin, lessons usually began at the age of seven and included both male and female pupils. Only boys went to school after age eleven, although relatively few continued their studies beyond this age. If a young man desired to continue his education, chances are his program of study would be completed before he reached the age of sixteen. Generally, only especially gifted boys, members of Rome's upper classes, and those considering a career in the Senate continued their education beyond the age of eleven.

Romans wrote on papyrus, the natural plant material that was used to make paper. The making of paper from papyrus was invented by the

This is a reconstruction of an ancient Roman library.

Egyptians around 1300 BC. Papyrus was available throughout the Roman Empire, and sheets were often formed into scrolls, some as long as thirty feet. Later, in the Christian era, papyrus was cut, folded, and sewn at the spine to form an eight-page book bound with wooden boards. This new invention was called a codex. Papyri were also sold in a rolled format, each about thirty-three feet in length. However, papyrus was expensive and could not be wasted; its use was restricted mostly to important documents and contracts.

Children who were learning to write used neither a papyrus roll nor a codex book. It was common for children of all ages to write Latin on wax tablets using a bronze or bone stylus, which was a pointed stick with one flattened end. Children would scratch or carve letters and numbers into the wax, which could then be smoothed over with the flat end of the stylus. In this way, the tablets could be reused.

Wax tablets were commonly bound together with leather. When they were closed, they would look like our journals do today. These tablets came in several different forms, each containing a different number of pages. For instance, a two-page tablet was called a diptych, a three-page tablet was a triptych, and a tablet with four or more pages was called a polyptychon. The wooden wax tablet was an early form of an item common in all classrooms today: the chalkboard.

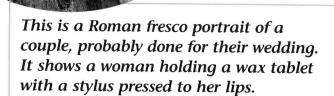

This is a Roman fresco portrait of a couple, probably done for their wedding. It shows a woman holding a wax tablet with a stylus pressed to her lips.

Roman students etched letters and numbers into wax tablets like these.

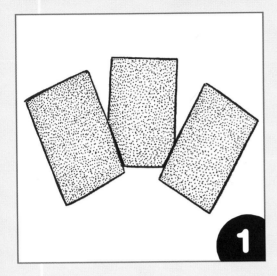

Wax Tablet*

Practice writing Latin just as children did in ancient Rome using a copy of a typical wax tablet.

* ADULT SUPERVISION IS REQUIRED FOR THIS CRAFT.

YOU WILL NEED

- Heavy cardboard
- Ruler
- Craft knife
- Scissors
- String or sisal twine
- Hole puncher
- White glue
- Toothpicks
- Craft paint
- Modeling clay
- Paintbrush

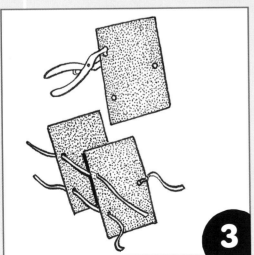

Step 1

Cut three equally sized rectangles from cardboard (approximately 5 by 7 inches).

Step 2

Use a ruler to draw a frame inside one of the rectangles. Cut and remove the center of the frame with a craft knife. Set the frame aside.

Step 3

Using a hole puncher, punch two holes along the edge of the second board, leaving a half-inch border. Also using the hole puncher, make one hole in the center of the opposite border. Use this board as a guide to mark and punch matching holes in your third piece of cardboard. This will be your tablet cover. Thread pieces of twine or string through each of the holes on the left, as shown. Take two additional lengths of string and tie them individually to the single holes on the right.

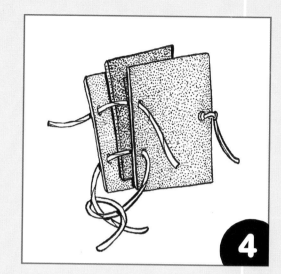

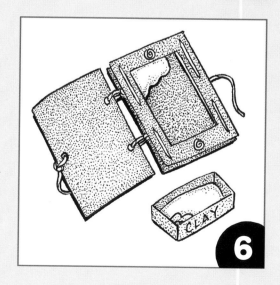

Step 4

Before tying the cover together, slip the "frame" board (from Step 2) between the two covers. Do this so the frame will fit within the book when it is glued in later. Tie both strings in tight, separate knots.

Step 5

Apply glue to the back of the frame and attach it to the inside of the book. When it dries, add decorative details by gluing toothpicks and twine to its cover. Paint the entire tablet whatever color you wish. Set aside to dry.

Step 6

To make a "wax" writing surface for your tablet, press small amounts of modeling clay into the frame's well. Flatten and smooth your clay writing surface. Now you can write Roman numerals or Latin words using a toothpick as your writing instrument. Erase your marks by flattening and smoothing the clay again.

Art and Architecture

Although much can be said of the wonders of Roman architecture, its advances could not have been realized without the innovations and discoveries of the Greeks before them. The one element that is unique to Roman architecture, however, is the dome, such as the one sitting atop the Pantheon, the Roman temple to all the gods.

Construction of the Pantheon began in 27 BC by the statesman Marcus Vipsanius Agrippa, and the original design did not include a dome. It was completely rebuilt by the emperor Hadrian sometime between AD 118 and AD 128, and the dome was added to the more traditional rectangular temple structure.

Because the Romans were able to mold constructions on the ground and then hoist them into place, decorative detail could become more elaborate. One such design element is the bronze

This view of the Pantheon shows natural light streaming through its dome.

rosettes and moldings that were placed into rectangular indentations cut into the ceiling. The dome, which has an opening in its very center, allows natural light inside the structure, illuminating its beauty. This opening also enables rainwater to fall inside, where it is collected and sent down a drain in the center of the floor, a feature commonly seen in many Roman buildings and homes.

Other architectural details, such as marble columns, arches, and vaults, were borrowed from the ancient Greeks and used to signal Rome's wealth and power. Arches are excellent supporting structures, and the Romans used them to great advantage, exploiting their simple design in everything from bridges and aqueducts to amphitheaters (which used arches to support the weight of thousands of the theaters' spectators). Arches developed a more distinctive, stately look when the Romans began to build triumphal arches to commemorate military victories, like the one built by Emperor Constantine in AD 315 to celebrate his victory over Emperor Maxentius.

Roman aqueducts, like this one in Spain, channeled drinking water to Romans throughout the empire.

The Arch of Constantine, a triumphal arch in Rome, dates from AD 315. It is inscribed, "Constantine overcame his enemies by divine inspiration."

Roman temples also resembled those built by the Greeks. Easily recognized by their row of columns running along the outer edge of the rectangular structures, most held a small inner room that only priests could enter. The public worshiped outside on the temple steps and altar. Many Roman temples, like other ancient structures built by the Romans (such as roads, bridges, and aqueducts), are still standing and are still in use today. They are enduring testaments to the strength and achievements of Rome's civilization.

Roman ruins in Pompeii

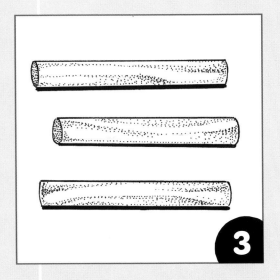

Roman Ruins*

Build a temple, the Pantheon, or other Roman ruins using columns, pediments, and capitals.

* ADULT SUPERVISION IS REQUIRED FOR THIS CRAFT.

YOU WILL NEED
- **Salt**
- **Cornstarch**
- **Water**
- **Baking sheet**
- **Blunt knife**
- **Toothpicks**
- **Black craft paint**
- **Paintbrush**

Salt Clay Recipe
2 cups salt
1 cup cornstarch
1 cup water

Mix ingredients in a medium-sized saucepan. Heat over a low flame for approximately five minutes, stirring constantly. Remove from heat once it thickens. Allow clay to cool for ten minutes before kneading.

Step 1
Mix the salt clay using the recipe on this page. You should make enough clay for approximately sixteen to twenty building pieces, depending on their size.

Step 2
Take small lumps of clay and roll them into balls. Make a deep thumbprint in the center of each ball. Add a few drops of black craft paint to the clay. Gently knead the clay, twisting it and folding it so that the black paint is mixed throughout and creates a marbled effect.

Step 3
Roll a few pieces of your marbleized clay between your palms until the clay forms sturdy, even-sized tubes. These will be your columns.

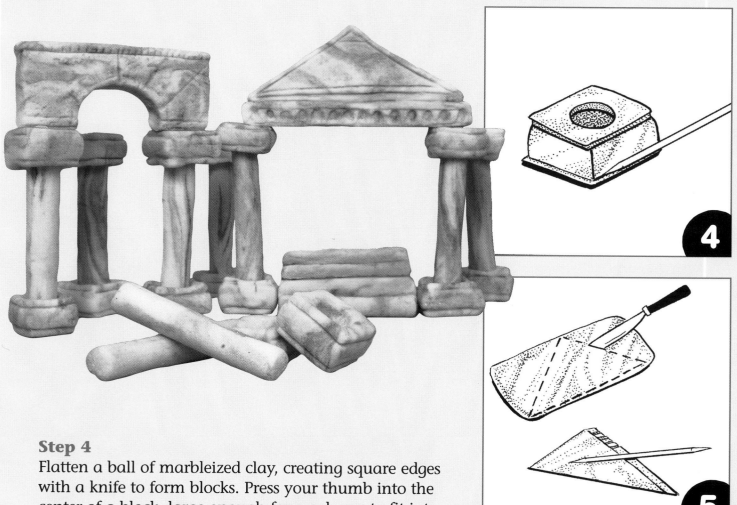

Step 4

Flatten a ball of marbleized clay, creating square edges with a knife to form blocks. Press your thumb into the center of a block, large enough for a column to fit into. This block will serve as the column's capital. Make six of these. Add detail by slicing horizontal lines in the sides of the capitals with a toothpick.

Step 5

Make large bricks by flattening lumps of clay in the same manner as you did to form the capitals in Step 4. Cut a triangular shape from the block to create a pediment. Decorate with toothpick lines along the two top edges.

Step 6

Set all of your building pieces on a baking sheet to dry for two to three days. Once fully dry, your blocks will be ready to be assembled into an ancient Roman structure.

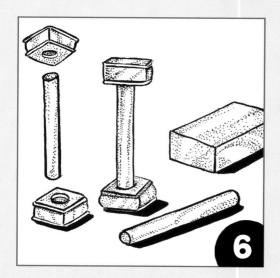

The Colosseum

The Colosseum was, and still is, symbolic of the Roman way of life. It celebrated the power of the Roman people, their leaders, and the empire itself. Like other forums in ancient Rome, the Colosseum was built so that its people could gather and be entertained by athletic feats and extreme violence.

The Games, as they were known, were held during the day and night (with the help of a huge, illuminated iron chandelier that was suspended above the stadium). The emperors themselves funded these events in an effort to gain the favor of the citizens and to keep them content and peaceful. The games often concluded with a series of gladiator fights, each one bloodier than the last.

Known to the ancient Romans as the Flavian Amphitheater, the Colosseum was a key destination for citizens interested in witnessing horrific entertainment of all kinds. Each visitor

This detail of a gladiator battling a leopard is from a Roman mosaic.

held a numbered ticket and sat in an assigned seat according to his or her rank in society. Senators and other important government officials sat in special seats in the first rows reserved just for them.

The Colosseum could hold some 50,000 visitors at one time, allowing the crowds ample room to enter and exit via its stairways and eighty arched, vaulted openings. Part of a collection of grand public structures that included the Circus Maximus—a U-shaped arena reserved for chariot racing—the Colosseum was the center of socially accepted and organized bloodshed in Rome. It was a place where an estimated 750,000 people—male and female slaves, criminals, and gladiators—met their deaths before supporters of Christianity stopped the brutal slayings. Death on its sandy floor often came in the form of hungry, savage lions and other dangerous animals. Led through a maze of narrow corridors under the main stage, these wild beasts were driven to kill each other or their human victims within the Colosseum walls on a daily basis. This senseless slaughter and reckless violence almost led to the extinction of several animal species during ancient times.

Lions were led through this maze beneath the wooden floor of the Colosseum to fight gladiators.

Named for the colossal statue of Nero that stands beyond its walls, the Colosseum was a project begun under the leadership of Emperor Vespasian during the year AD 72. It was finally completed by his son and heir, Emperor Titus, ten years later. Luxuries were added after its completion, such as a huge awning that protected viewers from the rain and hot sun.

The Colosseum's exterior was constructed of three tiers of arches and columns.

Colosseum Zoetrope

Design a small version of this ancient, once bloody arena that today sits quietly in the center of Rome.

YOU WILL NEED
- Photocopied pages
- Scissors
- Tape
- Cardboard
- Coffee can
- Pens or markers
- Pencil
- Craft paint (optional)
- Paintbrush (optional)

Step 1

Photocopy, trace, or electronically scan the chariot strip on page 31. Cut out the copied chariot strips. Use your scissors to remove each tiny slit at the top of each strip. Then create tiny flaps on the bottom of the strips by cutting along the lines that appear there.

Step 2

Draw or paint columns and vaulted arches on the blank side of your strips. To create a resemblance to the Colosseum, repeat the pattern illustrated in Drawing 2. Tape the strips together at the tabs on the end to form a ring with the chariot on the inside of the band.

Step 3

Trace the bottom of a coffee can on a piece of cardboard. Cut and remove it. Make a small hole in the center of the circle with the tip of a pen. Fold the flaps of the Colosseum to the underside of the circle and tape them to it.

Step 4

The zoetrope is finished. Put a pencil through the hole in the cardboard bottom. Spin it close to your eyes to view the chariot race in action.

Lives of the Emperors

This villa, built by Emperor Hadrian near Tivoli between AD 118 and AD 130, is one of the best preserved examples of ancient Roman architecture.

Rome became an empire after the murder of Julius Caesar in 44 BC. After his death, his son Octavian (later named Augustus) became Rome's first emperor and ruled with another leader, Mark Antony. Conflicts between the two led to a war in which Octavian emerged victorious following a famous sea battle in 31 BC. He was well-regarded by the Romans (just as Caesar had been before), and he ushered in a system of imperial rule that would last some 400 years. In 27 BC, after his victory over Mark Antony, he was renamed Augustus ("majestic") by the people. Rome was now an empire.

Roman emperors lived in a luxurious manner, from lavish housing to rich, elaborate meals. Unlike most Roman houses, their villas contained furnishings, indoor plumbing, and sometimes central heating. Many emperors lived in villas near the shore. These seaside retreats had interior baths, atriums to allow natural light indoors, and a series of smaller, private rooms organized around a courtyard. Like other homes, a villa fit for nobility contained beautiful frescoes and mosaic tiles as well as ornate woodwork. Masonry (stone) walls also surrounded most estates.

As a testament to their greatness, emperors often tried to top their predecessors by erecting more elaborate monuments to themselves and organizing spectacular and violent public entertainment. After an emperor won a war, for instance, he generally led his soldiers through the streets of Rome to great public acclaim while a slave standing behind him held a golden crown above the emperor's head. Trajan, an emperor who led Rome from AD 98–117, built a triumphal arch during his reign, after a successful military campaign that captured more territory for the empire, then at its peak. Julius Caesar made his mark as well: He was the first emperor whose likeness appeared on a Roman coin.

Almost every Roman emperor left behind some artifacts of his reign. These have contributed to the richness of Roman culture that we still marvel at today.

This detail from Trajan's Column depicts a battle scene. The 100-foot marble column held the emperor Trajan's ashes.

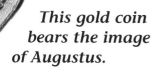

This gold coin bears the image of Augustus.

1

Portrait Coins

Make coins depicting Julius Caesar or the crowning of his son, Octavian, who was later renamed Augustus by the Roman people.

YOU WILL NEED
- Aluminum food container
- Bottle caps
- Ballpoint pen
- Scissors
- Toothpick
- Black craft paint
- Paintbrush
- Paper

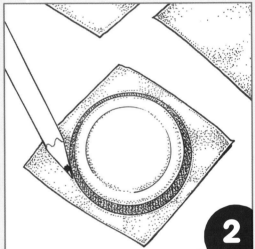

2

Step 1
Cut out the bottom of the flexible aluminum food container. Be careful—the edges can be sharp.

Step 2
Cut the piece into small squares, slightly larger than the bottle caps. With a ballpoint pen, press firmly into the foil as you trace the bottle caps onto the squares.

Step 3
Making simple lines, draw profiles of faces in the center of the circles using a pen or a toothpick. You can also trace magazine images onto the foil. Notice the raised lines you've made on the reverse side.

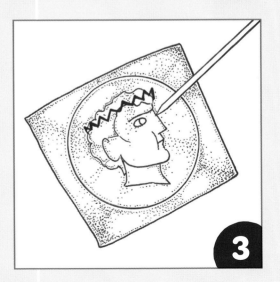

3

Step 4
Firmly press areas of the portrait you want to raise on the underside. Color in areas such as the ear, brow bone, nose, lips, chin, and cheekbone, as shown.

Step 5

Practice writing backwards on a piece of paper. Write the date in Roman numerals or names of emperors along the edge of the coin. Be sure that you write them backwards so you can read them on the embossed (or raised) side.

Step 6

With scissors, cut slits along the edge of the aluminum foil. Fold the tabs back onto the side you have drawn on to remove the sharp edge. Bring out the detail of your finished coins by rubbing a small dab of black craft paint onto the surface and then wiping most of it off for an interesting effect.

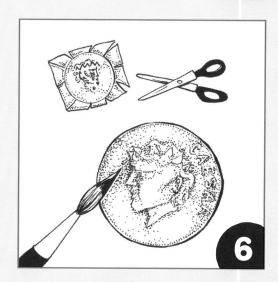

Decorative Arts

The Romans usually lived in sparsely furnished rooms, no matter what their lifestyle or position was in society. Decoration on the walls, however, was another matter. Many Romans hired skilled painters to depict mythological stories and scenes from daily life across the walls and ceilings of their homes. Some of these were even painted to look like windows and open arches, creating the illusion that the viewer is looking outdoors.

This kind of wall painting is known as trompe l'oeil ("fool the eye"), and is meant to make a room seem bigger than it is.

These kinds of wall paintings, in which paint is applied to wet plaster, are called frescoes. Paint applied to dry plaster is called tempera. There are many surviving examples of frescoes because the application of the paint to wet plaster served to preserve the pictures, enabling them to last for thousands of years.

Most of the painting styles and techniques used by the Romans were borrowed from the Greeks, who were master artists. Unlike today's artists who can use paint pigments straight from a tube, Roman artists had to make their own colors from natural substances. Most pigments were derived from mineral, vegetable, and animal sources, which were ground and then mixed with water or, in many cases, with raw eggs.

Some of the most famous Roman frescoes decorate the walls of homes in the ancient city of Pompeii. One is the Villa of Mysteries. This famous site includes a series of dramatic fresco paintings, representing certain stages of life and rites of passage. Hundreds of examples can still be seen by visitors, most depicting what life was like before the great eruption of Mount Vesuvius in AD 79.

The eruption of Mount Vesuvius killed an estimated 20,000 people in Pompeii in AD 79. Archaeologists discovered the ancient city in 1748 under nine feet of debris.

This detail is among the earliest examples of still-life painting. It is from the ancient city of Herculaneum, which, like Pompeii, was devastated by a volcanic eruption.

This fresco depicts a Roman woman playing the kithara, an ancient string instrument.

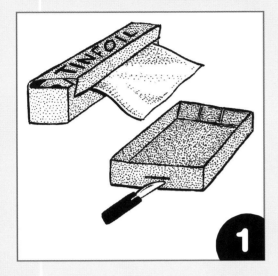

Fresco Painting*

Paint in the same style as the Romans did by copying this ancient technique.

* ADULT SUPERVISION IS REQUIRED FOR THIS CRAFT.

YOU WILL NEED
- Box top
- Aluminum foil
- Plaster of paris
- Tape
- Butterfly clip or large paper clip
- Gold craft paint
- Scissors
- Paintbrush
- Craft knife

Step 1
Line the bottom of a box top with aluminum foil. Make a small horizontal slit into one of the sides of the lid using a craft knife. This is where your picture hanger will go, so you must now decide if you want to make a horizontal or a vertical painting.

Step 2
Open a butterfly clip, or large paper clip, by bending it, as shown. Insert half of the clip into the slit and tape the sides of the slit closed to prevent plaster from seeping out.

Step 3
Mix the plaster according to the directions on the package. Ask a parent or a teacher to help you.

Step 4
Pour the plaster into the box top. Let it sit for several minutes to set.

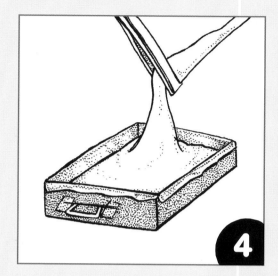

Step 5

Once the shiny surface of the plaster becomes dull, paint your design on it. Try to paint quickly. You will have only about eight to ten minutes to complete your picture. When the plaster starts to dry, stop painting. Your fresco is complete.

Step 6

When the plaster is completely dry, tear the box top away. Remove your fresco from the box. Paint the aluminum backing with gold craft paint if you desire. Once your paint has dried, the picture will be ready to hang on a wall.

Roman Craftspeople

There were many crafts-people in ancient Rome; most of them were male slaves or freedmen. Some had individual shops, such as the ones that have survived almost perfectly preserved in the city of Pompeii, but most worked near rich villas or city marketplaces. Some slaves and freedmen hoped to become rich through the perfection of their craft techniques.

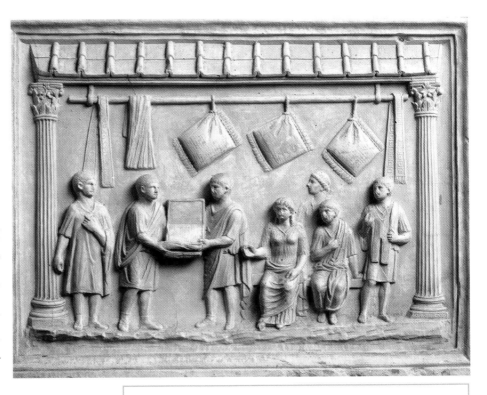

This Roman relief depicts a vendor of pillows and furniture coverings.

Most boys learned a skill or a trade such as glassmaking or metal-working from their fathers. Other boys studied as apprentice (student) workers. Romans often experimented with techniques and materials in order to create objects and treasures of great beauty.

One of the most popular trades was that of a potter. Amphorae, clay vessels, were used all over Rome to transport liquids such as wine, sauce, and water from place to place. They were designed to lean against walls, to be slender in form, and to carry large amounts of liquid. Amphorae are among the most common artifacts found by archaeologists who study the ancient Roman world. These discoveries have revealed that the clay vessels came in many shapes and sizes.

Because so many vessels have been discovered, archaeologists are certain that potters were rarely out of work in ancient Rome. Amphorae may have been mass-produced on farms where they were needed most to transport goods such as oil or wine for sale in distant markets. Before the liquids were packaged, the linings of the clay jugs had to be rubbed with a resinlike substance to make them waterproof, since clay is a porous material. They were then sealed with a stopper (a cork lid) held in place by cement and stamped with an identification of sorts, most likely the date and place of manufacture.

The Romans used more glass than any other ancient civilization, especially for common purposes, such as serving food and drinks.

Roman potters made many other clay objects. These included tableware, plates, bowls, oil lamps, figurines, tiles, and storage containers.

Most pottery, no matter where in Rome it originated, was made using a primitive form of a traditional potter's wheel, which was spun by hand. Pottery was often made from molds as well. The clay was hardened in much the same way as today's terra-cotta clays are, by being fired or heated at a high temperature, inside a kiln (an enclosed space like an oven).

These Roman jugs and architectural fragments were found in Pompeii.

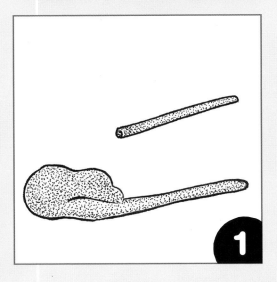

Amphora Vessel

Practice an ancient craft using clay, a common material often used by Roman craftspeople.

YOU WILL NEED
- Air-hardening clay
- Blunt knife
- Craft paint
- Paintbrush
- Clay modeling tools, such as Popsicle sticks, small spatulas, or kitchen utensils

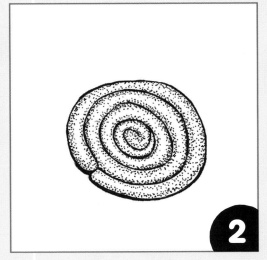

Step 1
Roll lumps of clay into long, slender lengths.

Step 2
Coil your clay into a circular shape to make the base of your vessel.

Step 3
Build up the sides of your vessel by stacking and attaching rows of rolled clay ropes. Join the clay rows from the inside of the pot by blending the clay with your fingers or any of the modeling tools listed above.

Step 4
Narrow your clay ropes as you reach the top, or neck, of your vessel. Use small rings of clay for the neck.

Step 5
Once you have finished the basic construction of your vessel, smooth the exterior surface with a blunt knife or another similar tool, or use your fingers. Hint: You may need to add a little water to help smooth the clay.

Step 6
Make handles for your vessel by rolling long tubes and attaching them to the sides using a toothpick or similar tool. Allow the vessel to fully dry, following the instructions on the package of clay. Once it is dry, paint it in any manner you wish.

TIMELINE

BC	3500	Egyptians develop first hieroglyphs.
	2575	Egypt's Old Kingdom begins. Great Pyramids and the Sphinx in Giza are started.
	776	First Olympic Games in Greece.
	510	Romans form a republic.
	449	Building of the Parthenon begins.
	336	Alexander the Great rules Greece.
	334	Alexander the Great invades Asia.
	332	Alexander the Great conquers Egypt.
	323	Alexander the Great dies. Greek Hellenistic period begins.
	147	Rome rules over Greece.
	49	Julius Caesar rules Rome.
	30	Egypt becomes a Roman province.
	27	Construction of Pantheon begins.
AD	5	Approximate birth of Jesus in Bethlehem.
	30	Jesus is crucified.
	43	Romans invade Britain.
	54	Nero becomes Rome's emperor and outlaws Christianity.
	70	Romans destroy Jerusalem. The Jews disperse to surrounding cities.
	72	Construction begins on the Colosseum in Rome.
	79	Mount Vesuvius destroys the Roman towns of Pompeii and Herculaneum.
	117	Roman Empire is at its greatest point.
	138	Plague, war, and famine create unrest in Roman cities.
	286	Roman Empire is divided.
	312	Emperor Constantine rules Rome and stops the persecution of Christians.
	330	Constantine makes Constantinople the capital of the Roman Empire.
	410	Roman Empire is reduced.

GLOSSARY

amphitheater Oval-shaped theater designed for entertainment such as gladiator fighting.

aqueduct Roman system of controlling water and supplying it to public fountains, bathhouses, and some homes.

archaeologist One who studies ancient civilizations by analyzing its objects.

artifact Object, especially a tool, made by human craftsmanship.

ballista Ancient Roman catapult used to hurl heavy stones as weapons.

bulla Amulet worn by Roman children until age fourteen to ensure safety.

circus Building for chariot racing.

city-state Town and its surrounding villages.

consul Top civil official of the Roman republic.

dictator Official who has complete authority, especially during a crisis such as war.

equestrian Business-oriented Roman landowner.

Etruscan Inhabitants of ancient Italy before the rise of the Roman Empire.

freedman/freedwoman Slave who has been freed.

frieze Long patterned band or picture used to decorate a wall.

infantry Group of 5,000 foot soldiers in the Roman army.

insula Multistory building with shops on its ground level and small rooms and apartments on the higher levels.

Isis Egyptian goddess of fertility sometimes worshiped by the Romans.

Jupiter Popular god and protector of Rome.

legion Largest unit in the Roman army.

nomadic Describing people who move from one settlement to another.

papyrus Natural Egyptian paper used throughout the ancient world.

patrician Roman elite who controlled politics in the Roman Empire.

plebeian Roman citizen who did not belong to the patrician class.

province Geographical area outside of Italy but part of the Roman Empire.

relief Sculpture that is raised from its flat background.

Senate Governing body of Rome during the republic.

stylus Roman writing tool made of bone or metal.

tablet Wooden boards coated with wax and used for writing.

villa Home for wealthy Romans.

FOR MORE INFORMATION

ORGANIZATIONS

Archaeological Institute of America
Boston University
656 Beacon Street, 4th floor
Boston, MA 02215-2006
Web site: http://www.archaeology.org

Boston Museum of Fine Arts
465 Huntington Avenue
Boston, MA 02115-5523
Web site: http://www.mfa.org

Metropolitan Museum of Art
1000 Fifth Avenue
New York, NY 10028
Web site: http://www.metmuseum.org

Smithsonian Institution Information Center
1000 Jefferson Drive SW
Washington, DC 20560-0010
(202) 357-2700
Web site: http://www.si.edu

World Archaeological Society
120 Lakewood Drive
Hollister, MO 65672

In Canada

Ontario Archaeological Society
11099 Bathurst Street
Richmond Hill, ON L4C 0N2
Web site: http://www.ontarioarchaeology.on.ca

WEB SITES

Dig! The Archaeology Magazine for Kids
http://www.digonsite.com

Illustrated History of the Roman Empire
http://www.roman-empire.net

Online Exhibition of Greek and Roman Art
(J. Paul Getty Museum of Art)
http://www.artsednet.getty.edu

Timeline: Ancient Rome
http://www.exovedate.com/
    ancient_timeline_one.html

FOR FURTHER READING

Guy, John. *Roman Life.* Hauppauge, NY:
    Barron's Educational Series, 1998.

Rees, Rosemary. *The Ancient Romans.*
    Des Plaines, IL: Heinemann Library, 1999.

Rogora, Bernardo. *The Romans.* Hauppauge,
    NY: Barron's Educational Publishers, 1999.

Simon, James. *Eyewitness: Ancient Rome.*
    New York: DK Publishing, 2000.

Simpson, Judith. *Ancient Rome.* New York:
    Time Life, 1997.

Steele, Philip. *Clothes and Crafts in Roman
    Times.* Milwaukee, WI: Gareth Stevens
    Publishing, 2000.

INDEX

ABOUT THE AUTHOR AND ILLUSTRATOR

Joann Jovinelly and Jason Netelkos have been working together on one project or another for more than a decade. This is their first collaborative series for young readers. They live in New York City.

PHOTO CREDITS

Cover artifact, p. 29 (bottom) © Philip & Karen Smith/SuperStock; pp. 4, 17 (bottom), 32, 37 (bottom right) © SuperStock; p. 5 © Huntington Library/SuperStock; p. 7 © Gianni Dagli Orti/Corbis; p. 8 © Roger Wood/Corbis; p. 10 © Charles & Josette Lenars/Corbis; pp. 12, 36 © Scala/Art Resource; p. 13 (top) © Allan T. Kohl/AICT; p. 13 (bottom) © Christie's Images/SuperStock; p. 16 © Richard T. Nowitz/Corbis; pp. 17 (top), 33 (top) by Leo C. Curran; pp. 20, 21 (top), 40 © Araldo de Luca/Corbis; pp. 21 (bottom), 41 (top) by Margaret M. Curran; p. 24 © Robert Zehring/Index Stock Imagery; p. 25 (top) © Gary Adams/Index Stock Imagery; p. 25 (middle) © Arte & Immagini srt/Corbis; p. 25 (bottom) © SteveVidler/SuperStock; p. 28 © Archivo Iconografico, S.A./Corbis; p. 29 (top) © Vanni Archive/Corbis; p. 33 (middle) © Vittoriano Rastelli/Corbis; pp. 33 (bottom), 41 (bottom) © Mimmo Jodice/Corbis; p. 37 (top) © Corbis; p. 37 (bottom left) © Museo Nazionale Archeologico, Napels/Canali PhotoBank, Milan/SuperStock; all craft illustrations and crafts by Jason Netelkos; all craft photographs by Adriana Skura.

SERIES DESIGN AND LAYOUT

Evelyn Horovicz

ACKNOWLEDGEMENT

Special thanks to Nicole Netelkos-Goetchius for her continued support.